Peter Oliver

Appendix to the Scripture lexicon

Peter Oliver

Appendix to the Scripture lexicon

ISBN/EAN: 9783337224509

Printed in Europe, USA, Canada, Australia, Japan

Cover: Foto ©Paul-Georg Meister /pixelio.de

More available books at **www.hansebooks.com**

P R E F A C E.

THE *Scripture Lexicon* being defigned for publick utility, the lefs incompleat it is, the defign of it will be better anfwered.

A few of the proper names in the *canon* of Scripture were omitted; and very many alfo which are in the *apocryphal* books, as having been judged to be of lefs confequence—but, upon further confideration, the compiler of the *Lexicon* hath thought proper to publifh the following *Appendix*; in which he hath inferted, almoft, if not, all the proper Names mentioned in the *Bible*—as alfo fome of the *jewifh* rites---together with the names and defcriptions of feveral *animals*, *plants*, &c. not commonly known to this part of the globe by their fcriptural names.

It will be obferved, that feveral names of perfons are inferted in the *Appendix*, which are already mentioned in the *Lexicon*; but as the fpelling, in the *Apocrypha*,

i3

is often different from that in the *canon* of Scripture, it was thought moft convenient to repeat them; and the *Lexicon* is generally referred to for the explanation of them.

At the end of this *Appendix* is added the interpretation of many names which were omitted in the *Lexicon*, but have, fince, been recovered—as alfo, an alteration of a few *accents*, which, upon revifal, it was thought proper to make—and an amendment of defcriptions under feveral names.

The compiler wifhes that there had not been any neceffity of correcting fo many errors ; but they being, chiefly, occafioned by unavoidable cafualties, he hopes, as they principally confift of *accents*, that the purchafer will be at lefs pains in altering them than if they were of a more tedious nature.

If this *Appendix* fhould tend to the more general utility of the *Lexicon*, it will add to the fatisfaction of the compiler, in having better anfwered his original defign.

APPENDIX

TO THE

SCRIPTURE LEXICON.

AB-A-DI'-AS. One who returned from the babylonish captivity.

AB-I-E'Z-RITE. *Ophrah* was a city of *Palestine* of the *Abiezrites*; probably descendents from *Abiezer*.

AB-I-SE'-I. An ancestor of *Esdras*.

A-BU'-BUS. An high-priest; the father-in-law of *Ptolomeus*, who betrayed *Simon Maccabeus*.

A before C.

A'C-COS. The grand-father of *Eupolemus*.

A'C-COZ. One whose sons returned from the babylonish captivity.

A'-CHAN (i. e. *troubling*; *gnashing*) A son of *Ezar* or *Ezer*, a descendant from the patriarch *Esau*.

A'C-I-PHA. One whose sons were servants of the temple.

A before D.

A'D-DUS. One whose sons returned from the babylonish captivity—also a servant of *Solomon*.

A-DI'-NUS. A *Levite* who returned from the babylonish captivity.

A.   A-DO'-

A-DO'-RA.   A place in the land of *Palestine*.
A-DU'-EL.   The great grand-father of *Tobit*.

A *before* E.

A-E'-DI-AS.   A porter or guard of the temple who returned from the babylonish captivity.

A *before* H.

A-HI'-SHAR.   See *Ahisham*.
A-HO'-HITE.   The descendents from *Ahoe* or *Ahoah*.
A-HO'-LI-BAH (i. e. *my tent or tabernacle is in her*) Jerusalem is so called by the prophet *Ezekiel*.

A *before* I.

A'-IN or AIN (i. e. *an eye* or *fountain*) A city of *Palestine* and one of the cities of refuge; first in the tribe of *Judah*, then in the tribe of *Simeon*.

A *before* L.

A'L-NA-THAN.   A principal man among the Jews after the babylonish captivity.

A *before* M.

AM-A'-DA-THUS.   See *Hammedatha*.
A'-MAL (i. e. *labour; iniquity*) A son of *Helem*, a descendent from the patriarch *Asher*.
AM-A-THE'-IS.   One who returned from the babylonish captivity.
AM-MI'-DI-OI.   A place mentioned in the *first* of *Esdras*, chap. v. ver. 20.
A'M-RAM-ITES.   The family of *Kohath*, descendents from *Amram*.

A *be-*

A *before* N.

A'-NA-EL. Brother to *Tobit* in the *Apocrypha*.

A'-NAN (i. e. *a cloud; prophecy; divination*) One who returned from the babylonifh captivity.

AN-A-N'I-EL. (i. e. *grace from God; grace of God*) The grand-father of *Tobit* in the *Apocrypha*.

A'-NES (i. e. *banifhment of grace*) See *Hanes*.

A'-NUS. A *Levite* who returned from the babylonifh captivity.

A *before* P.

A'P-PHUS. The furname of *Jonathan* the fon of *Mattathias*, in the *Apocrypha*.

A *before* R.

A-RA'-BI-ANS. The people of *Arabia* in *Afia*.

A'R-A-DUS. An inland city of the *Phœnicians*.

A'-RAM NA-HA-RA'-IM. Syria is called *Aram*, and *Naharaim* was a part of it lying between the rivers *Tigris* and *Euphrates*.

AR-BE'-LA. A city of *Affyria* in *Afia*; the country was called *Arbelis*, or *Arbelitis*.

A'RCH-ITES Inhabitants of *Archi*, a city of *Palefine* in the tribe of *Benjamin*.

A'-RES. One whofe fons returned from the babylonifh captivity.

A'R-NA. An anceftor of *Efdras*, in the *Apocrypha*.

A'ROM. One whofe family returned from the babylonifh captivity.

A'R-ZA. A fteward to king *Afa*.

A-SE'-AS. One who returned from the babylonifh captivity.

AS-E-BI'-A. See *Hafhabiah*.

A'SH-DOTH-ITES. Inhabitants of *Afhdod*, a diftrict of the *Philifines*.

A'-SHE-AN. A city of *Palefine*, in the tribe of *Judah*, in the mountains.

A 2   AS-

AS-I-BI'-AS. One who returned from the babylonifh captivity.

A'-SI-EL (i. e. *the work of God*) A fcribe mentioned in the *fecond* book of *Efdras*.

A'-SOM. One who returned from the babylonifh captivity.

ASS (*wild*) This animal inhabits the defarts of *Arabia*, as alfo *Africa* and *India*—it is now called the *Zebra*—it is a beautiful creature, and more refembles an horfc than an Afs; his cars are more like to thofe of an horfc than of an afs—he is well made, active and very fwift—he has fine legs; a tufted tail, and fmooth fkin—the males are white and brown, and the females white and black—the colours arc placed alternately in parallel lines, diftinct and narrow—he is ftreaked in that admirable manner, as to appear, at a diftance, as if covered with ribbons—he is larger than the common afs, and is fuppofed to be untameable, being very vicious.

AS-SA'-NI-AS. A prieft who returned from the babylonifh captivity.

A'S-SUR. The *Affyrians* are fo called—alfo one whofe fons were fervants of the temple.

A *before* T.

AT-E-RE'-ZI-AS. One whofe family returned from the babylonifh captivity.

A *before* Z.

A-ZA-E'-LUS. One who returned from the babylonifh captivity.

A'-ZA-RA. One whofe fons were fervants of the temple.

A'-ZAZ (i. e. *a ftrong one*) The father of *Bela*, a defcendent from the patriarch *Reuben*.

A'-ZEM. A city of *Palefine*, in the tribe of *Simeon*.

A-ZI-E'-I. An anceftor of *Efdras*.

A'Z-ZAH. A country of the *Avims*.

B.

B.

BA'-A-NA (i. e. *in affliction; anfwering*) One who returned from the babylonifh captivity.

BA-A-NI'-AS. One who returned from the babylonifh captivity.

BA'-BI. One who returned from the babylonifh captivity.

BAC-CHU'-RUS. A finger at the temple who returned from the babylonifh captivity.

BA-GO'-AS (i. e. *the inward; moft fecret; advanced; lifted up; bodily*) See *Bagoas.*

BA'-GO-I. One whofe family returned from the babylonifh captivity.

BA'-LAH. A city of *Palefline*, in the tribe of *Simeon.*

BA'-LA-NUS. One who returned from the babylonifh captivity.

BAL-NU'-US. One whofe fons returned from the babylonifh captivity.

BAN. One whofe fons returned from the babylonifh captivity.

BA'-NI. One whofe fons returned from the babylonifh captivity.

BA'-NID. One who returned from the babylonifh captivity.

BAN-NA'I-AS. One who returned from the babylo- captivity.

BA'N-NUS. One who returned from the babylonifh captivity.

BAN-

BA'N-U-AS. A *Levite* whofe family returned from the babylonifh captivity.

BAR-CE'-NOR. (i. e. *a drunkard,* or *wine-bibber*) An officer mentioned in the *fecond* book of *Maccabees.*

BA'R-GO. One who returned from the babylonifh captivity.

BA'S-CA-MA. A city of the land of *Gilead.*

BA'S-SA. One who returned from the babylonifh captivity with his family.

BA'S-TA-I. One who returned from the babylonifh captivity.

BATH-ZACH-A-RI'-AS. A place where *Judas Maccabæus* encamped againft *Antiochus Eupator;* not far from *Jerufalem.*

B *before* D.

BDE'L-LI-UM. A refinous gum, refembling myrrh, brought from the *Levant.*

B *before* E.

BE-DE'I-AH. See *Bedaiah.*

BE-E'L-SA-MUS. One who returned from the babylonifh captivity.

BE-E'L-SA-RUS. One who returned from the babylonifh captivity.

BE-E'-RA (i. e. *a well*; *declaring*) The fon of *Zophah,* a defcendent from the patriarch *Afher.*

BE'-HEM-OTH (i. e. *the multitude of earthly beafts*) It is much difputed, whether the *Hippopotamus* or *river horfe,* or the *Elephant,* is meant by *Behemoth*—the name, in Hebrew, fignifies *the* beaft or *greateft among beafts:* if fo, the *river-horfe* will not fupport that title; for it is faid, that in the rivers *Nile* and *Niger,* in *Africa,* they are not bigger than an afs; although *Thevenot* fays, that he faw one at *Cairo* in *Ægypt* as tall as a camel, and twice as large as an *ox:* but this was an uncommon phænomenon—but even this doth not equal the fize

of

of a full-grown *elephant*; for the common heighth of an *elephant* is ten feet and an half, and some of them are twelve feet high, and more—the mountains supply *him* with food; whereas the *river-horse* feeds chiefly on fish, and never goes far from the river—the *elephant* also retires to shady fenny places to cool himself—some of the *elephants* are called mountaineers; and they are called the *fen-animal* by some of the antients.

BE'-LAH (i. e. *destroying*) A son of the patriarch *Benjamin*.

BE'-LA-ITES. Descendents from *Belah*.

BEL-MA'-IM. A place of *Palestine*, not far from *Bethulia*.

BE'L-MEN. A place in the land of *Pa'estine*.

BE-RE-CHI'-AH (i. e. *speaking well of the Lord*) A door-keeper of the ark in king *David's* reign.

BE'-RITH. An ancestor of *Ezra*.

BE'-ROTH. See *Berothai*.

BER-ZE'-LUS. One who returned from the babylonish captivity.

BETH-SA-MOS. A place in the land of *Palestine*. See *Bethshemesh*.

BET-O-LI'-US. A place in the land of *Pa'estine*.

BE'-ZETH. A city of *Palestine* on the west side of the river *Jordan*.

B *before* I.

BI'-A-TAS. A *Levite* who returned from the babylonish captivity.

BI'L-HAN (i. e. *old; troubled*) A son of *Ezar*, a descendent from the patriarch *Esau*—also a son of *Jediael* a descendent from the patriarch *Benjamin*.

BO'C-CAS. An ancestor of *Esdras*.

C.

C.

CA'B-BON (i. e. *as though underſtanding*) A city of *Paleſtine* in the tribe of *Judah* in the *valley.*

CA'D-DIS. A name of *Joannes* the ſon of *Mattathias* in the hiſtory of the *Maccabees.*

CA'L-A-MUS (i. e. *ſweet)* It is called *ſweet cane* by the prophet *Jeremiah*—it is a ſpicy root, belonging to a ruſh or flag.

CA'L-COL (i. e. *nouriſhing*; *or as conſuming all things*) A ſon of *Zerah* a deſcendent from the patriarch *Judah*. See *Chalcol.*

CA'L-PHI. The father of *Judas* in the Apocrypha.

CA'M-EL. A large quadruped of ſeveral ſpecies— the *Camel*, which is the largeſt ſize, chews the cud, but divides not the hoof—he has a ſtomach to hold water, which, by a contraction of its muſcles, he can throw into his ſtomach which contains its dry food ; and by means of the firſt mentioned ſtomach he is able to travel through the ſandy deſerts of *Africa* and *Aſia,* for a long time, without a freſh ſupply of water—he is covered with a fine fur, ſhorter and ſofter than that of the ox-kind — he hath two bunches on his back ; and about the bunches there grow hairs nearly a foot long—it is an excellent beaſt of burden, and ſome of them will carry *twelve* or *thirteen hundred pounds* weight on their backs ; for which load he kneels, being *ſeven* or *eight* feet
high

high; or more—they travel flow ; though there is a fpecies of them very fwift.

The *Dromedary* is of the camel-kind, but hath only one bunch on his back.

CAMP, or ENCAMPMENT of the *Ifraelites*.

The encampments of the *Ifraelites* muft have been a grand piece of fcenery. The whole body of the people, confifting of *fix hundred thoufand* fighting men, befides women and children, was difpofed under *four* battalions, fo placed as to enclofe the *tabernacle,* in the form of a fquare, and each under one general ftandard. Military men, well verfed in tacticks, admire their method of encampment, which was firft imitated by the *Greeks* and afterwards by the *Romans*.

There were *forty-one* encampments from their *firft* (in the month of *March)* at *Ramefes* in the land of *Gofhen* in *Ægypt* and in the *wildernefs*, until they reached the land of *Canaan* : they are thus enumerated in the *thirty-third* chapter of *Numbers*.

1. At *Ramefes*.
2. *Succoth*.
3. *Etham* on the edge of the wildernefs.
4. *Pihahiroth*.
5. *Marah*.
6. *Elim*.
7. By the *Red Sea*.
8. *Wildernefs* of *Sin*.
9. *Dophkah*.
10. *Alufh*.
11. *Rephidim*.
12. *Wildernefs* of *Sinai*.
13. *Kibroth-hattaavah*.
14. *Hazeroth*.
15. *Rithmah*.
16. *Rimmon-parez*.
17. *Libnah*.
18. *Riffah*.
19. *Rehelathah*.
20. *Shapher*.
21. *Haradah*.
22. *Mackheloth*.
23. *Tahath*.
24. *Tarah*.
25. *Mithcah*.
26. *Hafhmonah*.
27. *Moferoth*.
28. *Bene-jaakam*.
29. *Hor-hagidgad*.
30. *Jotbathah*.
31. *Ebronah*.
32. *Ezion-gaber*.
33. *Kadefh* or the wildernefs of *Sin*.
34. Mount *Hor*.

B

35. *Zal-*

35. *Zalmonah.*
36. *Punon.*
37. *Oboth.*
38. *Ije-abarim.*

39. *Dibon-gad.*
40. *Almon-diblathaim.*
41. Mountains of *Abarim.*

In the fecond year after their *Exodus* from *Ægypt*, they were numbered; and upon an exact poll the number of their males amounted to *fix hundred and three thoufand, five hundred,* and *fifty,* from *twenty* years old and upwards.

CA-PHI'-RA. See *Chephirah.*

CA'PH-TO-RIM. A fon of *Mifraim.*

CAR-A-BA'-SI-ON. One who returned from the babylonifh captivity.

CA'R-CHA-MIS. See *Carchemifh.*

CA-RE'-AH (i. e. *bald; ice*) The father of *Johanan* who joined with *Gedaliah,* and was made a governor in *Judah* by *Nebuchadnezzar* king of *Babylon.*

CA'-RI-A. A province of *leffer Afia,* which fubmitted to the *Romans* under *Antiochus,* about 198 years B. C.

CAR-MA'-NI-ANS. A people of *Carmania,* a province of *Perfia.*

CA'R-ME. A prieft who returned from the babylonifh captivity with his family.

CA'R-MITES. A people who defcended from *Carmi* a fon of the patriarch *Reuben.*

CA'R-NI-ON. A ftrong city of *Gilead,* mentioned in the *fecond* book of *Maccabees,* and taken by *Judas Maccabæus.*

CA'S-PIS or CA'S-PHIN. A ftrong city of *Syria,* on the eaft fide of the river *Jordan.*

CA'S-SIA. An aromatick plant, of which *Arabia* produced the beft fort.

C *before* E.

CEI'-LAN (i. e. *diffolving that*) One whofe family returned from the babylonifh captivity.

CEL-

CEL-E-MI'-A. A fcribe mentioned in the *fecond* book of *Efdras*.

CE'-TEB. One whofe fons were fervants to the temple.

CE'-RAS. One whofe fons were fervants to the temple.

C *before* H.

CHA'-BRIS. One who was a governor of *Bethulia*.

CHA'-DI-AS. A place mentioned in the *firft Efdras*, chap. v. ver. 20.

CHA-MO'IS. Suppofed to be the *Arabian goat*, called the *mountain goat*.

CHA'R-CUS. One whofe fons returned from the babylonifh captivity, and were fervants of the temple.

CHA'RM-ER. Suppofed to be one who is an aftrologer or confulter of the ftars, in order to divination or foretelling future events.

CHA'R-MIS. One who was a governor of *Bethulia*.

CHA'-SE-BA. One who returned from the babylonifh captivity.

CHE'-LAL (i. e. *as night*) A fon of *Pahath-Moab*.

CHE'L-CI-AS (i. e. *the portion or gentlenefs of the Lord*) The father of *Sufanna*, in the Apocrypha.

CHE'-LOD. One mentioned in the book of *Judith*.

CHE'R-UB (i. e. *as a mafter*; *as a child*; *as fighting*) A city of the babylonifh empire.

CHE'T-TI-IM. See *Chittim*.

CHO'-BA. A place in the land of *Palefine*.

CHU'S-I. A place in the land of *Palefine*.

C *before* I.

CI-SA'-I. An anceftor of *Mardocheus*, or *Mordecai*, of the tribe of *Benjamin*.

CI'T-TIMS. The people of *Perfia* fo called.

C *before*

C *before* O.

CO'CK-A-TRICE. A venemous ferpent of the oviparous kind, in *Afia* and *Africa*—it is fometimes called a *bafilifk*, of which many fabulous ftories are told.

CO'L-LI-US or CA'-LI-TAS. A *Levite* who returned from the babylonifh captivity.

COR. An *hebrew* meafure; the fame as *Homer*.

CO'R-BE. One who returned from the babylonifh captivity.

CO'-RE. See *Korah*.

CO'R-MO-RANT. A fpecies of the *pelican*, almoft as large as a goofe, with fourteen long feathers in its tail; the under part of the body is whitifh—it is a fea-fowl and lives upon fifh, and dives very rapidly after its prey—the *hebrew* and *greek* name of this bird is cxpreffive of its impetuofity.

C *before* R.

CRO'C-O-DILE. See *Leviathan*.

C *before* Y.

CY'M-BAL. A brafs inftrument of mufick, fomething like to a kettle drum, but fmaller.

D.

D.

DA'-BRI-A. A fcribe mentioned in the *fecond* book of *Efdras*.

DAD-DE'US. One who returned from the babylonifh captivity.

DAI'-SAN. One whofe fons were fervants of the temple.

DA'-RI-AN. One who returned from the babylonifh captivity.

D *before* E.

DE'-DA-NIM (i. e. *the beloved of thofe*) Uncertain whether he was a defcendent from *Japhet* or *Ham*.

DE'-LUS or DE'-LOS. An ifland in the *Ægean* fea, reputed to be the birth place of *Apollo* and *Diana*.

DE'-MO-PHON (i. e. *flaying the people*) A governor appointed by *Antiochus*; in the Apocrypha.

D *before* I.

DI'-AS-CO-RI'NTH-I-US (i. e. *an heavenly ornament*) Suppofed to be the name of a *Corinthian* month, about our *March* or *April*.

DI'S-CUS. A game among the *Athenians*, by throwing a round piece of iron or other metal, or a ftone a ſtone, with an hole in the center : it depended upon ſtrength and ſlight to throw it to the greateſt diſtance : it was like our game of *quoits*.

D *before* O.

DO′-CUS.   An hold or fortreſs built by *Abubus* the father of *Ptolemy* ; in *ſecond* book of *Maccabees*.

DOVES DUNG.   It is ſaid in the *ſecond* book of *Kings*, chap. vi. ver. 24, that, in the famine of *Samaria*, the fourth part of a cab of *doves-dung* ſold for five pieces of ſilver or near *two ſhillings* ſterling.   There is ſome diſpute what is meant by *doves·dung ;* ſome ſuppoſe it to be the real excrement of the dove—others, that it was the contents of the crop of the dove ; but *Bochartus* ſays, that the *Arabians* have a kind of vetches or lentiles called *doves-dung* ; which was the cheapeſt of food.

D *before* R.

DRO′M-E-DA-RY.   See *Camel.*

E.

E.

E-A'-NAS. One who returned from the babylonifh captivity.

E *before* C.

E-CA'-NUS. A fcribe mentioned in the *fecond* book of *Efdras*.

E *before* D.

E'-DES. One who returned from the babylonifh captivity.

E *before* K.

E'K-RE-BEL. A place in the land of *Pa'eftine*.

E *before* L.

E'L-AH. A duke of *Edom*; alfo an officer of king *Solomon*; alfo a fon of *Caleb*.

E'L-CI-A (i. e. *the portion or gentlenefs of the Lord*) An anceftor of *Judith* in the Apocrypha.

E'L-EPH (i. e. *learning*) A city of *Paleftine* in the tribe of *Benjamin*.

EL-I'-A-DUN. One who returned from the babylonifh captivity.

EL-I'-AH-BA. A *fhaalbonite* one of king *David's* worthies.

EL-I'-A-LI (i. e. *God's afcenfion*) One who returned from the babylonifh captivity.

EL-

EL-I'S-I-MUS. A porter or guard of the temple; one who returned from the babyloniſh captivity.

E'L-I-U. Grandfather to *Elkanah* the father of *Samuel.*

E'L-ON-ITES. Defcendents from *Elon,* of the poſterity of the patriarch *Eſau.*

E *before* M.

E'M-MER (i. e. *ſaying*; *ſpeaking*; *a lamb*) One who returned from the babyloniſh captivity.

E *before* N.

EN-CA'MP-MENT. See *Camp.*

E *before* P.

E'PH-ER (i. e. *duſt or lead*) A fon of *Midian* and grandfon of the patriarch *Abraham.*

E'PH-RATH (i. e. *abundance or fertility*) A wife of *Caleb.*

E *before* S.

E-SE-BRI'-AS. A prieſt who returned from the babyloniſh captivity.

E-SO'-RA. The name of a place in *Paleſtine.*

E'SH-BAN (i. e. *fire of the ſun*) A defcendent from the patriarch *Eſau.*

E *before* T.

ETH-MA. One whoſe fons returned from the babyloniſh captivity.

E *before* U.

EU'-NA-TAN. A principal man among the *jews* after the babyloniſh captivity.

E *before*

E *before* X.

EX-O'R-CIST. Is one who hath the power of cafting out devils, or difeafes. This power was given by our *Saviour* to his difciples ; which they exercifed for the benefit of mankind; and is fuppofed to have continued about 200 years in the chriftian church. This power was alfo pretended to by others, and indeed, is ftill arrogated by the *church of Rome*, in which, the exorcift, after many ceremonies, re-peats thefe words, *viz*. " I exorcife thee, unclean " fpirit ! in the name of *Jefus Chrift :* tremble, " O *Satan !* thou enemy of the faith ! thou foe " of mankind! who haft brought death into the " world, who haft deprived men of life, and haft " rebelled againft juftice ; thou feducer of man-" kind! thou root of evil! thou fource of avarice, " difcord, and envy"!—the *romanifts* alfo exor-cife houfes and other places, fuppofed to be haunted by unclean fpirits.

E *before* Z.

E'ZAR. A fon of *Seir*, a defcendent from the patri-arch *Efau*.

EZ-E-RI'-AS. The grandfather of *Efdras* in the Apocrypha.

E-ZI'-AS. An anceftor of *Efdras*.

E'Z-RIL. One who returned from the babylonifh captivity.

C F.

F.

FAT VALLEY. The vallies in the tribe of *Ephra-im*, in the land of *Palestine*, were so called from the richness and fertility of their soil.

F *before* E.

FEASTS. The *jews* observed sundry festivals—as, the feast of unleavened bread or the *passover*. See *Passover*. The feast of *tabernacles*. See *Tabernacles*. The feast of *weeks* or *pentecost*. See *Pentecost*. The feast of *trumpets*, which was celebrated on the first and second day of the month *Tisri*, or the first month of the civil year—the *jews* in general believe that it was instituted in memory of the creation, which, they say, was in that month—some say, that it was in memory of *Isaac*'s deliverance from being sacrificed—others, that it was in commemoration of the law being given from mount *Sinai*, when the trumpet and thunder were heard—and others, that it was in preparation, to put mankind in mind of the *general resurrection*, which is to be ushered in by the sound of a trumpet—but the most probable reason seems to be, the proclaiming the entrance of the *civil* year ; as all contracts, mortgages, &c. were to be regulated by it.

The feast of the *new moons* was observed on the first day of every moon ; and those who observed

or

or thought they obferved the *new moon*, were to repair with all fpeed to the grand council, and give notice of it : and according to the credibility of the witneffes, the prefident proclaimed the *new moon* by found of trumpet. All thefe feafts were obferved by facrifices.

The foregoing feafts were appointed by the *mofaic* law ; but in procefs of time, the *jews* added others : as the feaft of *Purim* or of *lots,* in memory of their deliverance from *Haman*'s cruelty —alfo the feaft of the *dedication* of the temple ; and others.

F *before* X.

FOX-ES. It is by n⁰ means probable that thofe animals which in facred writ are called *foxes,* were of the fame fpecies which are *now* called *foxes*—the hebrew word *Shual,* tranflated *fox,* will comprehend other animals, and perhaps all other beafts of prey of the fame fize—thefe creatures were exceeding numerous in *Judæa,* and feveral places received their names from them, as *Hazar - Shual, the gate of the fox, &c.*—they went together in large herds, fo that two hundred have been feen in a company, whereas *our* fox is not a gregarious animal—befides, they were very fond of grapes, and deftroyed the vineyards ; in allufion to which is that verfe in chap. ii. of *Solomon's fong,* viz. *take us the foxes, the little foxes, that fpoil the vines : for our vines have tender grapes.*

F *before* R.

FRONT-LET. It was wore on the *forehead.* See *Fronthet.*

G.

G A'B-A-THA. An eunuch of *Artaxerxes* king of *Perſia*.

GA'D-DES. The name of a place in *Paleſtine*.

GA'L-GA-LA. A city of *Aſſyria* in *Aſia*.

GA-MA'-EL. A ſon of *Ithamar*.

GAR. One of the ſervants of *Solomon*.

G *before* E.

GE'D-DUR. One whoſe ſons were ſervants of the temple.

GEN-NE'-US. The father of one of the *Appollonius's*, an oppreſſor of the *jews*.

GE'-SEM. See *Goſhen*.

G *before* I.

GI'-ER EA'-GLE. It is the *vulture-eagle*, a bird between the vulture and the eagle: *gier* is the old engliſh word for *vulture*.

G *before* L.

GLEDE. A bird of the *kite* ſpecies.

G *before* O.

GOAT *(ſcape)* The goat which was ſet at liberty on the day of ſolemn expiation (among the *jews)* bearing

bearing away or efcaping with the fins of the people. See *Azazel.*

GOR-TY'-NA. An inland city of the ifle of *Crete.*

GO-THO'N-I-EL. Father of *Chabris* a governor of *Bethulia.*

G *before* R.

GRA'-BA. One whofe fons were fervants of the temple.

H.

HA'-DAR (i. e. *power; greatnefs*) A king of *Edom.*

HA'G-A-BAH (i. e. *a grafshopper*) See *Agaba.*

HA'-GA-I. A fervant of *Solomon.*

HA'G-GAI. A fon of the patriarch *Gad.*

HAI or HA'-I. See *Ai.*

HARP. An inftrument of mufick with feveral ftrings, to be played upon with the fingers.

HA-SHU'-BAH (i. e. *eftimation or thought*) A defcendent from king *David.*

HA'V-I-LAH. Alfo fuppofed to be a part of *Arabia.* See *Havilah.*

H *before* E.

HE'-MAN. A defcendent from the patriarch *Efau.*

HE'-PHER. Alfo a country. See *Hepher.*

HE'R-

HE'R-ON. A fierce bird of the *eagle* kind, which feeds upon fish.

HEA'VE OFFERINGS. See *Offerings*.

H *before* I.

HI-E'-RE-EL. One who returned from the babylonish captivity.

HI-E'R-E-MOTH (i. e. *he that fears, sees, or rejects death*) One who returned from the babylonish captivity, and was a porter or guard of the temple. See *Jerimoth*.

HI-ER-I-E'-LUS. One who returned from the babylonish captivity.

HI-E'R-MAS. One who returned from the babylonish captivity, and was a guard or porter of the temple.

H *before* O.

HO'-LEN. A city of refuge in the land of *Palestine*. See *Helon*.

H *before* U.

HUL (i. e. *sorrow*; *iniquity*; *sand*) A son of *Aram* and grandson to *Shem* the patriarch.

J I.

JA-AZ-I'-EL (i. e. *the strength of the Lord*) One who was a porter or guard of the temple.

JA'-BESH (i. e. *draught ; confusion*) The father of *Shallum* who usurped the throne of *Judah.*

JA'-BEZ (i. e. *sadness ; sorrow ; grief*) One mentioned in the *first* Chron. chap. iv. ver. 9—also a city *first* Chron. chap. ii. ver. 55, perhaps *Jabesh-Gilead.*

JA'-CU-BUS. A *Levite* who returned from the babylonish captivity.

JA'M-BRI (i. e. *rebellious ; waxing bitter ; changing*) By the children of *Jambri* is meant, a people of *Arabia* who were plundering robbers.

JA'M-NA-AN. A place mentioned in the Apocrypha.

JA'-SA-EL. One who returned from the babylonish captivity.

JA'-TAL. One whose sons were porters or guards of the temple.

I *before* D.

I-DU'-EL. A principal man among the *jews* after the babylonish captivity.

I-DU-MÆ'-ANS (i. e. *red ; earthy ; bloody*) The people of *Idumæa.*

J before

J *before* E.

JE-BU'-SI. Alſo a border of the tribe of *Benjamin* in the land of *Canaan*. See *Jebuſi*.

JED-DE'-US. One who returned from the babyloniſh captivity.

JE'D-DU. A prieſt who returned from the babyloniſh captivity with his family.

JE-E'-LI. One of the ſervants of *Solomon*.

JE-HA'-LE-EL (i. e. *praiſing God*; *the clearneſs of God*) One of the porters or guards of the temple.

JEH-DEI'-AH (i. e. *joy*; *together*; *one Lord*) A *Meronothite* who had the care of the *aſſes* in king *David*'s reign.

JE-HO'-A-DAH (i. e. *the congregation*; *paſſing over*; *the teſtimony or taking away of the Lord*) The ſon of *Achaz*, of the poſterity of king *Saul*.

JE'R-I-BAI (i. e. *fighting*; *chiding*; *multiplying*) Alſo one who returned from the babyloniſh captivity. See *Jeribai*.

JE'-SU-A. An high prieſt of the *jews*. See *Jeſus*.

I *before* G.

I'-GAL. Alſo a prince of the tribe of *Iſſachar*. See *Igal*.

J *before* O.

JO'-A-CHAZ (i. e. *the preparing or ſtability of the Lord*) The ſon of king *Joſias*, *firſt* Eſdras, chap. i. ver. 34; the ſame with *Jehoahaz*.

JO'-AH. Alſo the ſon of *Aſaph* the recorder; and others. See *Joah*.

JO-A'N-NAN. The ſon of *Mattathias*, in the Apocrypha.

JO-A-ZA'B-DUS. A *Levite* who returned from the babyloniſh captivity.

JO'-DA. One who returned from the babyloniſh captivity.

JO'-

JO'-RAM (i. e. *the heighth or throwing down of the Lord*) A captain over thoufands under king *Jo-fiah*—alfo a fon of *Toi* king of *Hamath*.

JO-SA-PHI'-AS (i. e. *the increafe of the Lord; the Lord finifhing*) One who returned from the babylonifh captivity.

JO'-SE-EL. One who returned from the babylonifh captivity.

JO-SI'-PHUS. One who returned from the babylonifh captivity.

I-O'-TA. A letter of the *greek* alphabet; fignifying fmallnefs or the leaft part of a thing.

I *before* S.

I'S-DA-EL. One of the fervants of *Solomon*.

J *before* U.

JU'-DAS (i. e. *confeffion; praife*) A *Levite* who re-turned from the babylonifh captivity.

JU'-EL. One who returned from the babylonifh cap-tivity.

JU'-NIA. A kinfwoman to St. *Paul.* See *Junia*.

D

K.

K.

KIR-I-A-THA'-RI-US. The name of a place in the land of *Palestine*.

KITE.   A species of the *Falcon*, with a forked tail, a brown body, and a whitish head; and about the size of a large tame pidgeon.

K *before* N.

KNOPS. Ornaments of a round figure, like to apples or pomegranates.

L.

LA'-BA-NA (i. e. *the moon*; *whiteness*; *frankincense*) One who returned from the babylonish captivity, and whose sons were servants of the temple.

LA-CU'-NUS. One who returned from the babylonish captivity.

LA-

LA'-DAN (i. e. *the fame as Laadan*) One who returned from the babylonifh captivity.

LA'P-WING. A bird about the fize of a common
pidgeon, with a piercing eye, a fmall beautiful
head, elegantly variegated and ornamented with
a beautiful creft hanging over the hinder part of
the neck—it is a bird almoft continually on the
wing, and feeds upon infects.

I. before E.

LE'P-RO-SY. A filthy and infectious difeafe, par-
ticularly defcribed in the book of *Leviticus* ; but
is not that which is *now* called the leprofy—it
infected walls and wood of houfes, and garments,
which is fuppofed to have proceeded from infects.

LE'T-TUS. One who returned from the babylonifh
captivity.

LE-VI'-A-THAN (i. e. *a coup'ing together ; his fellow-
fhip)* The *Leviathan* is generally fuppofed to be
intended for the *wha'e*; and is really meant fo in
the 104th *Pfalm :* but in the 74th *Pfalm* and in
the 27th chapter of the prophet *Ifaiah* it means
the *crocodile,* as emblematical of the *Ægyptians*
whofe river *Nile* abounded with *crocodiles*—but
more efpecially in the book of *Job,* the *crocodile*
feems to be intended ; as the defcription of the
leviathan, there, anfwers to the character of the
crocodile, but by no means is defcriptive of the
whale.

The river *Nile* in *Ægypt* is remarkable for
crocodiles. It is an amphibious animal ; it hath
four legs ; its upper parts are covered with im-
penetrable fcales, like to a coat of mail—it is generally about eighteen feet long, and fome are much
longer---it is an oviparous animal; but its multi-
plication is leffened by the *ichneumon,* an animal
of the *rat* kind, who devours its eggs.

LE'.VIS. One who returned from the babylonifh
captivity.

LO-

L *before* O.

LO'-CUST. The *locuſt* is a large winged infect, in ſhape like to a graſshopper; very common in *Europe*, *Aſia* and *Africa*—*Thevenot*, the traveller, ſays, that they live about ſix months, and lay about 300 eggs in autumn, which are hatched in the following ſpring—it is ſaid, that in *Arabia* the whole air hath been darkened by their flight for 18 or 20 miles—they devour the fruits of the earth in a very rapid manner, ſo as to occaſion a famine. In *Aſia* and *Africa* it is common for people to eat them, and to preſerve them in ſalt and pickle, and in ſeveral other ways—the common way of dreſſing them, was by plucking off their legs and wings and then putting them over a blaze, in a pan full of holes; or elſe, to knock them down and lay them in heaps, and then kindle a fire about them---it is ſuppoſed that *John the baptiſt* made this ſort of locuſts a part of his food in the wilderneſs.

LO'Z-ON. One who was a ſervant to *Solomon*.

M.

M'A-A-NAI One who returned from the babyloniſh captivity.

MA'B-DA-I. One who returned from the babyloniſh captivity.

MA'CH-

MA'CH-MAS. or MI'CH-MASH See *Michmas*.

MA'-CRON. A furname of one of the *Ptolomies*.

MA-DI'-A-BUN. One who returned from the babylonifh captivity.

MA-E'-LUS. One who returned from the babylonifh captivity.

MA'-GI. Suppofed to be philofophers who ftudied aftronomy: The *Chaldeans* were well fkilled in that fcience, and it was their wife-men, who having obferved the new ftar at our *Savior*'s birth, waited upon the new born infant with their offerings.

MA-GI'-CIAN. One who deals in divination, pretending to know the fecrets of futurity—the word fignifies, *to fee fecrets*.

MA'-HA-LATH MA'S-CHIL. The words in the title of the 53rd. *Pfalm*—the word *mahalath* fignifies a flute or pipe ; and *mafchil* the tune or fong.

MA'-HA-LI. (i. e. *infirmity ; ficknefs ; an harp ; pardon*) A fon of *Merari*. See *Mahli*.

MAI-A'-NE-AS. A *Levite* who returned from the babylonifh captivity.

MA'-KAD. A city of *Palefline*.

MA'-KAS (i. e. *an end ; ending ; waxing hope*) A place of *Palefline* where one of king *Solomon*'s officers refided, who had the care of the provifions for the royal houfhold. See *Mahuz*.

MA'L-LAS. A place mentioned in the *fecond* book of *Maccabees*.

MA-MA'I-AS. A principal man among the *jews*, who returned from the babylonifh captivity.

MA-NAS-S'E-AS. One who returned from the babylonifh captivity.

MA'-NI. One whofe fons returned from the babylonifh captivity.

MA'N-NA. A fweet dew, which, through the coolnefs of the night and morning, was congealed into little corns like coriander feeds—the hebrew word which we tranflate *manna* is a queftion viz. *what is this?* for the *Ifraelites* had no name for it ; for
they

they wift not what it was; and therefore afked
this queftion.

MA-RI'-SA. See *Marefhah*.

MA'R-MOTH. A prieft who returned from the babylonifh captivity.

MA'-SE-LOTH. A city of *Affyria*.

MA'S-MAN. A principal man among the *jews* after
their captivity.

MA'S-MOTH. A prieft who returned from the ba-.
bylonifh captivity.

MAS-SI'-AS. One who returned from the babylonifh
captivity.

MAT-THE'-LAS. A jewifh prieft who had married a
ftrange wife during the babylonifh captivity.

M *before* E.

ME-A'-NI One who returned from the babylonifh
captivity.

MEA'S-URE. A *jewifh* meafure was about eight
bufhels and an half.

MEA'T OFFERING. See *Offerings*.

ME-E'D-A. One whofe fons were fervants of the
temple after the babylonifh captivity.

ME'-HA-LI. See *Mahli*.

ME-HU'-NIMS. A people who dwelt on the borders
of *Ægypt*.

MEL-CHI'-AS One who returned from the babylonifh captivity.

ME'L-CHI-EL (i. e. *God is my king*) Father of *Char-
mis* a governor of *Bethulia*.

ME-NE'S-THE-US. (i. e. *chearfulnefs*; *anger*; *or the
ftrength of God*) The Father of *Apollonius*, in the
fecond book of *Maccabees*.

ME'-NITH. One who returned from the babylonifh
captivity.

ME'R-AN. A city of *Arabia* in *Afia*.

ME'R-CY SEAT. The cover of the ark of the covenant, or cheft, in which were depofited the tables
of the law : it was covered with pure gold, and
two

two golden cherubims ſtretched forth their wings to cover it; one at each end.

ME'-RI-BAH KA'-DESH. A place where the *Iſraelites* murmured in the wilderneſs.

ME'-RUTH. A *prieſt* who returned from the babyloniſh captivity with his family.

ME'-SECH. (i. e. *prolonging*; *drawing*; *or hedging in waters*) Suppoſed not to be a place; but the meaning of the word is, *how long?*—ſome ſay, it was a country taking its name from *Meſheck* the ſon of *Japhet*.

ME'-SHA. (i. e. *a burden*; *a taking*; *ſalvation*) A place mentioned in the book of *Geneſis*; the dwelling of the ſons of *Joktan*.

ME-TE'-RUS. One who returned from the babyloniſh captivity with his family.

ME'-ZA-HAB. The mother of *Matrid*. See *Mezahab*.

M *before* I.

MI'-CHAH. (i. e. *poor*; *lowly*) A ſon of *Uzziel* and father of *Shamir*.

MI'N-STREL. Is one who can play well upon an inſtrument of muſick.

M *before* O.

MO'CK-RAM. A river of *Paleſtine*.

MO'.ETH, A *Levite* who returned from the babyloniſh captivity.

MO'LI. A ſon of *Levi*.

MO'M-DIS. One who returned from the babyloniſh captivity.

MO-SO'L-LAM. One who returned from the babyloniſh captivity. See *Meſhullam*.

MO-SU'L-LA-MON. A principal man among the *jews*, after the babyloniſh captivity.

M *before* U.

MUTH-LA'B-BEN. A word in the title of the 9th *Pfalm*, fuppofed to be an inftrument of *mufick*, but uncertain what.

M *before* Y.

MY'N-DUS. A city of *Lower Afia*.

N.

N *before* A.

NA'-A-THUS. One who returned from the ba- bylonifh captivity.

NA-BA'-RI-US. One who returned from the baby- lonifh captivity.

NA-DA'-BA-THA. A place in *Arabia*.

NA'-I-DUS. One who returned from the babylonifh captivity.

NA'PH-THAR (i. e. *a cleanfing*) A flame fo called in the 2d book of *Maccabees*. See *Nephi*.

NA'S-BAS. A nephew to *Achiacarus*, the cup- bearer to *Sarchedonus* king of *Affyria*.

NA'-SITH. One whofe fons were fervants of the temple.

NA-THA-NI'-AS. One who returned from the baby- lonifh captivity.

NA'-VE. (i. e. *a pofterity; fairnefs; remaining for ever*) The fame perfon as *Jofhua*.

N *before* E.

NE'-CRO-MAN-CER. One who enquires of the dead, or a confulter of dead idols—their manner of confulting the dead, was, by vifiting their graves in the night, and there laying and muttering certain words with a low voice; by which means they pretended to have communion with them by dreams, or by their appearing to them.

NE'PH-I. The place where *Nehemiah* found the muddy water, which was in the pit where the holy fire had been hid. 2nd *Maccabees*, chap. i. ver. 36. See *Naphthar.*

NE'PH-IS. One who returned from the babylonifh captivity with his family.

NE'PH-TA-LI (i. e. *the fame as Naphtali*) A city of *Paleftine* in *Galilee*, near to *Thifbe.*

NE'-RO. An emperor of *Rome* who began to reign A. D. 54, and killed himfelf June 8, A. D. 68, Æt. 32, after a reign of 13 years, 7 months and 28 days—he firft perfecuted the chriftians A. D. 64—in his reign A. D. 67, St. *Paul* was beheaded and St. *Peter* crucified at *Rome.*

NE-TO'-PHAH. One who returned from the babylonifh captivity with his family.

N *before* I.

NILE. See *River of Ægypt.*

N *before* O.

NON (i. e. *fon; pofterity; everlafting; a fifh*) A fon of the patriarch *Ephraim.*

E   O.

O.

O'-BETH. One who returned from the babylonifh captivity.

O'C-I-NA. A place mentioned in the book of *Judith*.

O'F-FER-INGS. Among the *jews*, under the mofaic law, there were a variety of offerings inftituted, which are accurately defcribed in the beginning of the book of *Leviticus*, as

    Burnt-offerings : thefe were to confift, either of the herd, and out of that the bullock only and he without blemifh—or of the flock, as the fheep or the goat, and out of that the male only, and he without blemifh—or laftly, of fowls, the turtle dove or the young pidgeon—thefe *five* were the only offering for a burnt facrifice, which was to be wholly deftroyed by fire, and at the door of the tabernacle only; except what was thrown away of the legs and infides of the bullock, fheep or goat, and the crop and feathers of the birds. There was no unclean beaft or bird to be offered —and thefe were to be offered by way of atonement for fin. *Philo*, the learned jew, obferves, that the offerer was to be like his oblation; if fo, then induftry and innocence, ufefulnefs and fimplicity are recommended, by this inftitution, to the worfhippers of GOD.

    Drink-offerings. With a *bullock, half a hin of wine*, with three tenth deals of flour and half a hin of oil.

With

With a *Ram, one third of an hin of wine,* with two tenth deals of flour and one third of an hin of oil.

With a *lamb* or a *kid* of the *goat, one quarter of an hin of wine,* with one tenth deal of flour and one quarter of an hin of oil.

With a *sheaf of the first fruits, one quarter of an hin of wine,* with one tenth deal of flour with oil.

Heave-offering. It is so called, from the sacrifice its being lifted up towards heaven in token of its being devoted to GOD.

Meat-offering. It might well be translated *wheat-offering,* as it consisted, chiefly, of *flour;* for no fort of flesh was to be offered in it—it consisted of things inanimate, as *flour, bread, oil, wine, salt, frankincense,* &c.—the wave sheaf and the two wave loaves for the whole congregation, and the others for private persons according to their ability in the expence of their offering—the bread was to be *unleavened,* for *Maimonides* says, it was to distinguish the worshippers of the true GOD from the *Zabian* idolaters of those times, who offered to their gods no bread but *leavened.*

Peace-offering. It was an offering of thanksgiving for peace, or for mercies received---sometimes it was offered by way of *vow,* in hope of peace or future blessings; and sometimes it was offered without any antecedent obligation of a vow, in which case it was called a *free-will-offering.* The *sin* and *trespass-offering* supposed the offender obnoxious, and GOD displeased; but the *peace-offering* supposed GOD to be reconciled to the offerer, and him to be at peace with GOD. In the *sin* and *trespass-offering,* though the priests partook of it, yet the offerer had no share; but in the *peace-offering* both priest and offerer partook and feasted upon it. In the *burnt-offering* or *holocaust* the whole sacrifice was consumed by fire, and neither priest or offerer partook of them.

E 2

Sin-

Sin-offering. Sin-offerings were for expiation of particular fins or legal imperfections, called therefore, *fin-offerings*—the firft fort were for fins of ignorance or furprize, either by the high-prieft or body of the community, by the rulers, or by any one of the common people. The other fort of fin-offering was for *voluntary* fins; but as to the more capital violations of the *moral* law, as for *murder*, *adultery*, or the *worfhip of idols*, no expiatory facrifice was admitted.

Trefpafs-offering. It was for concealing the knowledge of a thing, as a witnefs ; for touching an unclean thing ; or in making a rafh oath---the offender, in this cafe, was to offer a female from the flock, a lamb or a kid ; or two turtle-doves or two young pidgeons---but if the trefpafs related to *holy things*, then the trefpaffer was to offer a ram without blemifh.

Wave-offering. It was fo called, becaufe it was waved *up* and *down*, and *eaft*, *weft*, *north* and *fouth*, to fignify that he to whom it was offered, was Lord of the whole world, the GOD who fills all fpace, and to whom all things of right belong.

There were *annually* facrificed at the *national* charge

1201 Lambs
132 Bullocks
72 Rams
21 Kids
2 Goats

befides *voluntary*, *vow* and *trefpafs* offerings.

ON-I'-A-RES. The name of a *Lacedæmonian* officer.

O'-NUS. One who returned from the babylonifh captivity.

ON-Y'-CHA. An aromatic plant of *Arabia :* fome take it to be *bdellium*.

O'S-PRAY. The *fea eagle*, a bird of prey, very ftrong and fwift.

O'S-

O'S-SI-FRAGE. A fpecies of *eagle*, fo called from its breaking the bones of its prey, which it carries high in the air, and then lets it fall upon a rock.

O'S-TRICH. An *african* bird, wild, and of the fhape of a goofe, but much larger---it is very tall, fo that, fometimes, they are tutored to carry a perfon upon their backs---It is ufually *feven feet* high from the top of the head to the ground, the neck being about three feet of the *feven*---when the neck is ftretched out in a right line, he is about *fix feet* from head to tail, and the tail is about *twelve inches* long---the wings are fhort but ftrong- it is very fwift of foot, and its wings help in running, but it cannot fly---the plumage is black, white or grey---it devours almoft any thing, even metals, but as to its digefting iron, it is fabulous--- it is bred in dry defarts, and the female lays its eggs in the fand, ten or twelve together, as large as a common bowl---it is faid that fhe is fo forgetful as not to remember the place where fhe lays them, fo that when fhe comes to any place where there are eggs, fhe fits upon them and hatches them---when they are hunted, they run with fuch velocity and ftrength fo as to fling the ftones behind them which annoy their purfuers.

O *before* U.

OU'CH-ES. *Ouches* are the fockets in which ftones are fet in any metals.

O *before* Z.

OZ-O'-RA. One who returned from the babylonifh captivity.

P.

PALM-TREE. The *Palm-Tree* is a tall ſtrait tree, growing ſometimes to the height of an hundred feet---it is common in *Africa*; and from its trunk the natives extract a liquor called *palm-wine*, reſembling whey in colour, but very ſweet---it is extracted by making an inciſion at the top of the trunk, to which they apply *gourd-bottles*, into which the liquor runs by pipes made of its leaves- the wine is purgative when new; but if kept two or three days, it ferments, grows ſtrong, and is palatable and wholeſome---the *leaves*, which are large, ſerve for the coverings of houſes---palm-trees are common alſo in *Aſia*; and *Jericho* was called *the city of palm-trees*·

PA-TRO'-CLUS (i. e. *of the father*; *the glory of the country*) The father of *Nicanor* in the 2nd book of *Maccabees*.

PE'L-I-AS. One who returned from the babyloniſh captivity.

PE'L-I-CAN. A bird both of *Aſia* and *Africa*—it is in the ſhape of and as large as a *ſwan*, and ſome of them much larger; the beak and feathers ſomething

fomething fimilar—it hath a flefhy bag at its
throat to hold provifions for its young, large
enough to contain a man's head—it frequents
frefh and falt waters, forefts and groves—it principally feeds upon fifh and water infects—it builds
its neft in groves or bufhy places—after having
fed itfelf, it then feeds its young, who eat out of
the bag at its throat; from whence arofe the vul-
gar error that its young fed on its blood.

P *before* H.

PHA'I-SUR. One who returned from the babylonifh
captivity.

PHAL-DAI'-US. One who returned from the babylonifh captivity.

PHA-LE'-AS. One whofe fons were fervants of the
temple.

PHA'R-ZITES (i. e. *divided*) A family defcended
from *Pharez*.

PHA'-SI-RON. A place, or people, mentioned in
the *firf* book of *Maccabees*.

PHI-LA'R-CHES (i. e. *the lover of a prince*) One who
was an affociate with *Timotheus*, in the *fecond* book
of *Maccabees*.

PHI-LO-ME'-TOR (i e. *a lover of the mother*) A
furname of one of the *Ptolomie's*.

PHO'-ROS. One who was a porter or guard of the
temple, after his return from the babylonifh captivity.

PHRY'-GI-A PA-CA-TI-A'-NA. A diftrict of *Phry-
gia* in *Afia*, of which *Laodicæa* was the capital: it
was fo called from *Pacatianus* who was the roman
prefect of it under the emperor *Conftantine*.

P *before* I.

PI'-RA. A place in the land of *Palefline*.

P *before* O.

POME'-GRAN-ATE. A fruit of the fize of a large *apple*, growing in various parts of the world; the covering is hard and the pulp agreeable, with many hard feeds in it—the hem of the jewifh *high-prieft*'s garment was to be adorned with the figures of *pomegranates*.

POS-I-DO'-NI-US (i. e. *giving drink*) One of the officers of *Seleucus Nicanor*.

P *before* R.

PROPH-ET. In more antient times a prophet was called a *feer*. The *prophets* or *feers* were thofe who foretold future events which were difcovered to them in dreams or in vifions, by divine infpiration ; although fome of them were falfe prophets or pretenders to divine infpiration—they were a fociety by themfelves, and had an head prefiding over their fchool—they lived in the country, retired—they dreffed very plain, mean and coarfe--- they were very bold in their addreffes to all orders of men---from their coarfe drefs and addrefs they were often accounted *mad-men*.

P *before* Y.

PY'-GARG. An animal of the *goat* kind.

Q.

Q _before_ U.

QUAILS. The _Quails_ mentioned in facred writ; which fell around the camp of the _Ifraelites_ in the wildernefs, arc fuppofed by _fome_ to be _locufts_, which are in great flights to this day, and arc ufed as food; and, by fome, thought to be delicious food—by _others_ they are thought to be a bird which travels in vaft flights to this day; fome think, of the _blackbird_ kind---perhaps they might be of that kind which are now called _wild-pidgeons_; for in _New Mexico_, and almoft in all _North America_, thofe pidgeons were, not long fince, fo numerous, that they fometimes concealed the fun in their flight: and it is too well known to be denyed, that a flight of them hath continued as it were in a ftring for a long time, for the length of _twenty_ miles and more---the exprcffion of _feathered fowl_ made ufe of by the _Pfalmift_, feems to favour the opinion of their being _birds_, as _locufts_ have no feathers.

R.

R *before* A.

R A'B-BITH. One of the border towns of the tribe of *Iffachar* in *Palefline*.

RA'-HAB· *Lower Ægypt* is fo called by the *Pfalmift* and by *Ifaiah*.

RA'-MA-THEM (i. c. *high; caft away*) A government of *Samaria* added to *Judæa*.

RA'-PHA-IM. An anceftor of *Judith*, in the *Apocrypha*.

RA'-ZIS (i. e. *the fecret or myftery of the Lord*) An elder of *Jerufalem* after the babylonifh captivity.

R *before* E.

RE-E-LI'-AS. See *Reelaiah*.

RE'-PHA-IM. A piace of *Palefline*, in whofe valley *Saul* encamped againft *David*.

R *before* I.

RI'V-ER OF Æ'-GYPT. Now, the river *Nile*; as taking this name from *Nilus* one of the antient kings of *Ægypt*—It is called in facred writ, *the river of Ægypt,* as the river *Euphrates* is there called the *great river.*

The

The river *Nile* is much noted in antient hiftory-it was firft called *Oceanus;* then *Aetus* or *Aqui'a;* afterwards *Ægyptus* and generally fo by *Homer;* and afterwards *Triton,* from the three former names: at laft, the *Nile.*

This river rifes in *Abyffinia* from two fmall fprings about a ftones throw from each other, the larger being about two feet diameter; but being joined by many rivers emptying into it, it runs meandring many hundred miles, until it empties into the *mediterranean fea.*—The fertility of *Ægypt* is owing to the overflowings of this river---there are what they call *Nilometers,* to meafure the rifing of the river; it is faid, that the prefent *Nilometer* is a large fquare refervoir furrounded by a gallery for the obfervers of the rife of the river to walk on---in the midft of this refervoir or bafon is an octagonal pillar of marble, divided into parts and marked---a canal is cut from the river to this refervoir, by which is feen daily the rife of the river —fome fay, if it rifes only about *eighteen* or *twenty feet* a famine enfues, but if it exceeds *twenty-four* or *twenty-five* feet it doth great damage: though others make the lownefs and the height of the waters materially different. The river begins to rife about *midfummer,* and ceafes to rife in *Auguft,* and falls in *September.*

The *Sphinxes* were deftined to fhew at what time of the year the waters began to rife—they were a fymbolic figure, with the head of a *woman* and the body of a *lion,* fignifying that the *Nile* began to fwell in the months of *July* and *Auguft,* when the fun paffes through the figns of *Leo* and *Virgo*—feveral of thefe *fphinxes* are ftill to be feen; one of which, fays *Thevenot* the traveller, is 26 feet high, and 15 feet from the ear to the chin; but *Pliny* fays, the head was 102 feet about, and 62 feet above the belly; that the body was 143

feet

feet long, and was thought to be the fepulchre of king *Amafis*.

R *before* O.

RO-I'-MUS.   One who returned from the babylonifh captivity.

S.

S *before* A.

SA'-BAT.   One of the fervants of *Solomon*.

SA'-BA-TUS.   A porter or guard of the temple after the babylonifh captivity.

SA'B-BAN.   One who returned from the babylonifh captivity.

SAB-BE'-US.   One who returned from the babylonifh captivity.

SA'-BI.   A fervant of *Solomon*.

SA-DA-MI'-AS.   An anceftor of *Efdras*, in the *Apocrypha*.

SA'-DAS.   One who returned from the babylonifh captivity with his family.

SAD-DE'-US..   A jewifh captain in the treafury office, who returned from the babylonifh captivity.

SA'D-DUC.   An anceftor of *Efdras*, in the *Apocrypha*.

SA'-

SA'-LOM (i. e. *peace*) Grandfather of *Joachim* the high-prieſt of the jews—the father of *Chelcias*, in the *Apocrypha*.

SA'-LUM. A porter or guard of the temple after the babyloniſh captivity.

SA'-MA-EL. An anceſtor of *Judith*, in the *Apocrypha*.

SA-MAI'-AS (i. e. *hearing or obeying the Lord*) One who returned from the babyloniſh captivity.

SA-MEI'-US. One who returned from the babyloniſh captivity.

SA'-MI. One whoſe ſons were porters or guards of the temple.

SA'M-MUS. One who returned from the babyloniſh captivity.

SA'MP-SA-MES. A place mentioned in the 1ſt book of *Maccabees*.

SAN-A-BA'S-SA-RUS. A ruler among the *jews* after the babyloniſh captivity.

SA'N-DALS. At firſt were only *ſoles* tied to the feet with ſtrings : afterwards, *ſhoes* were called *ſandals*.

SA'-PHAT. One whoſe ſons returned from the babyloniſh captivity.

SA-PHA-TI'-AS. One who returned from the babyloniſh captivity.

SA'PPH-ETH. One who was a ſervant of *Solomon*.

SA-RAI'-AS (i. e. *my prince of the Lord*; *or the ſong of the Lord*) A prieſt who returned from the babyloniſh captivity; the father of *Joſedec* and of *Eſdras*.

SAR-DE'-US. One who returned from the babyloniſh captivity.

SA'-RE-A. A *ſcribe* mentioned in the ſecond book of *Eſdras*.

SATH-RA-BA'Z-NES. A ruler in *Syria*. See *Sathrabcuzanes*.

SA'-TYRS. Some tranſlators call them *wild bucks*, which inhabit deſart places—ſome call them *apes*, and *wild goats*.

SA'-VI-AS. An anceſtor of *Eſdras*, in the *Apocrypha*.

S be-

S *before* E.

SECH-EN-I'-AS. One who returned from the baby-lonish captivity.

SEERS. See *Prophets.*

SEL-E-MI'-AS. One who returned from the babylo-nish captivity.

SE'M-IS. A *Levite* who returned from the babylonish captivity.

SEPH-E'-LA. The southern part of the plain of *Jezreel.*

SE'-SIS. One who returned from the babylonish captivity.

SE'ST-HEL. One who returned from the babylonish captivity.

SHAM-A-RI'-AH (i. e. *the keeping ; hardness or throne of the Lord)* One ot king *Rehoboam's* sons.

SHEW BREAD. So called becaufe expofed to public view before the *ark.*

SHI'M-E-ATH-ITES. A family of the *fcribes,* fkil-led in prophecies.

SHIT-TAH TREE (i. e. *a thorn)* A tree mention-ed in *Ifaiah,* chap. 41, ver. 19, the word *puxos* which our tranflators have rendered *Shittah-tree,* is the *greek* word for the *box-tree.*

SHO'-BAL. A fon of *Seir* the *Horite.*

S *before* I.

SI'C-Y-ON. A city of *Peloponnefus* in *Greece:* it was fo called, and the whole *Peninfula* of *Peloponnefus* was called *Sicyonia,* from *Sicyon* its *nineteenth* king: originally it was called *Ægialia,* from *Ægialus* its firft monarch.

SI'-DE. A maritime city of *Pamphylia* in *Afia.*

SI-FI'N-NES. A governor of *Cæle* Syria or *hollow Syria.*

SI'-RACH (i. e. *an hiffing ; a fong of the brother ; an empty gift)* The father of *Jefus* in the *Apocrypha.*

S *before* P.

SPI'KE-NARD. It is the *nardus* or *nard* brought from the *Eaſt Indies*, and from *Alexandria* in *Ægypt* —it is an aromatic plant of a moſt fragrant perfume.

S *before* T.

STO'-RAX. It is a dry, ſolid *reſin*, of a reddiſh colour and fragrant ſmell—it is produced from a tree which grows in *Syria* and in the *Eaſt Indies*.

STORK. A bird of the ſize of a *crane*, or about 3 feet high---its colour is white and brown---the nails of its feet reſemble a man's nails---its bill is long and jagged---it has long and red legs---it feeds on ſerpents, frogs, &c. in marſhy places--- it lays but four eggs and ſits upon them thirty days---it is remarkable for its *filial piety*. One of the ſeven wiſe men of *Greece* being aſked by *Cræ-ſus* king of *Lydia*, which was the moſt happy animal? anſwered, *the ſtork, becauſe it performs what is juſt and right by nature, without any compulſive law.*

S *before* U.

SU'-BA. One of the ſervants of *Solomon*.

SU'-BA-I. One whoſe ſons were ſervants of the temple.

SUD (i. e. *my ſecret*) One whoſe ſons were ſervants of the temple.

SU'-DI-AS. A *Levite* who returned from the babylo-captivity.

SUR (i. e. *giving back*; *rebellion*) A place mentioned in the *Apocrypha*. See *Shur.*

SU' SA (i. e. *an horſe*; *a ſwallow*; *a moth*) The metropolis of *Perſia* in *Aſia.*

S *before* Y.

SYN'-A-GOGUE. Buildings for public worfhip a-
mong the *jews*—it is faid, that there were no
fynagogues erected, until after their return from
the babylonifh captivity—but it feems to be probable, that thofe, who lived at a diftance from
Jerufalem, where the temple worfhip was held,
muft have had fome other place to worfhip in
than in the open air.

T.

T *before* A.

TA'CH-ES. The *taches* of the *tabernacle* were
hooks, buckles, or clafps ufed for its curtains.

TA'L-SAS. A *prieft* who returned from the babylonifh captivity.

TA'-NIS (i. e. *a motion ; moving or moved*) A city of
Ægypt.

TENTH DEAL. A *jewifh* meafure containing between three and four quarts *englifh* meafure.

TE'-TA. One who returned from the babylonifh
captivity.

T be-

T *before* H.

THA'-RA. One mentioned in St. *Luke's* genealogical list.

THA'R-RA. An eunuch of *Artaxerxes* king of *Perfia*.

THA'S-SI (i. e. *forgetful; a debtor)* The furname of *Simon* the fon of *Mattathias,* in the *Apocrypha.*

THE-CO'-E (i. e. *hope*; *alive*; *congregation)* A wildernefs near to the *dead fea* or *lake of Sodom.*

THEL-E'R-SAS (i. e. *an heaping up of deafnefs*; *the wood of dolefulnefs)* A place in the babylonian empire.

THE'R-AS. A river mentioned in the *Apocrypha.*

THI'S-BE. A city of *Galilee* in the land of *Canaan.*

THO-MO'-I. One whofe fons were fervants to the temple.

THRA-SE'-AS. (i. e. *the fame as Tarfhifh)* The father of *Apollonius* in the fecond book of *Maccabees.*

T *before* I.

TI'-GRIS (i. e. *the fharpnefs of fwiftnefs; a fharp found*; *a voice*; *one only fwiftnefs)* See *Tigris* in *Lexicon.*

TI'M-BREL. An inftrument of mufick much ufed among the *jews,* of the *drum* kind, to be beat upon to caufe a found.

T *before* U.

TU-BI-E'-NI (i. e. *ftraw*; *arfwering well)* Certain *jews* fo called, in the 2nd book of *Maccabees,* from their living in the land of *Tob* or *Tubin* which lay on the northern fide of *Manaffeh's* lot, on the other fide of the river *Jordan.*

G   V.

V and U.

V *before* I.

V I'-OL. A ftringed inftrument of mufick, among
the *jews*, to be played upon with a bow, as a
violin is.

U *before* N.

Unclean and clean Animals.

Under the *mofaick* conftitution various kinds
of animals were *prohibited*, and other kinds *allowed*, for food. The reafons for which were *moral*,
political, and *natural*—the two former in order to
preferve the *jews*, as a diftinct people, from the
idolatrous nations, in the worfhip of *one God*, only, as hath been already hinted in the cafe of
unleavened bread.

The *natural* reafon for the prohibition might
be, that the prohibited animals were of an al-
kalefcent nature and fo productive of various
difeafes in the hot climate of *Judæa*, agreeable to
the remarks of a noted englifh-phyfician—more
efpecially the *fwine*, which feeds upon all manner of filth, and, as divers writers of note have
obferved, is apt to breed the *leprofy* in warm cli-
mates

mates, and other *scrofulous* diforders; the word *scrofula* being derived from the latin word *scrofa*, a *sow* : the *swine* being fubject to the *leprofy* and the *meafles*, proceeding from its bad feeding.

The mofaick rule was, *among beafts*, that whatever *parted the hoof, was cloven footed and chewed the cud*, was allowed to be eaten : thofe that were *prohibited* are thus claffed in the 11th chaper of *Leviticus*, viz.

The *Camel*
 Cony which is fuppofed to be a fpecies of rat,
  beween a cony and rat, common in *Ægypt*
  and *Paleftine*
 Hare
 Swine

Prohibited Fish

Were thofe, which have not *fins*, nor *fcales*.

Prohibited Fowls.

The *Bat*
 Cormorant
 Cuckow
 Eagle
Fowls that creep, going
  on all fours, as
  Bats and all kinds
  of *Flies*
The *Gier Eagle*
 Hawks
 Heron

The *Kite*
 Lapwing
 Night-hawk
 Ofpray
 Offifrage
 Owl
 Great and little owl
 Pelican
 Raven
 Stork
 Swan and *Vulture*

Thofe

Thofe which go on their paws, on *all* fours, were
prohibited, viz.

The *Chamelion*	The *Moufe*
Ferret	*Snail*
Lizard	*Tortoife*
Mole	*Weafel*

The following were accounted *clean*, viz.

All flying creeping things which go upon *all* fours,
and have legs above their feet to leap with, as

The *Bald-Locuft*.
Beetle, fuppofed to be another fort of *Locuft*
Grafshopper
Locuft

U'-NI-CORN. It is an animal having but *one* horn,
and mentioned in feveral places in *facred writ*. It
is by many fuppofed to be fictitious; as there is
no land animal, now known, of that kind : although there is a fifh, called a *fea unicorn*, as having an horn projecting from its nofe, parallel
with its body. That mentioned in the book of
Job, is thought, by fome, to be meant the *wild
bull* of *Arabia*, as the hebrew name of it is *Reem*,
which is mentioned in feveral places of facred
writ as of the *beeve* kind—but, father *Lobo*, the
portuguefe jefuit, fays, that when he was in
Abyffinia, towards the beginning of the laft cen-
tury

tury, he faw an *unicorn,* but could not come near to him—he defcribes it, as having the fhape of a beautiful *horfe,* exact and nicely proportioned, of a bay colour, with a black tail, which, he fays, in fome provinces is long, in others fhort: fome have long mains hanging to the ground—they are timorous, and never feed but when they are furrounded with other animals to defend them—it is alfo faid, that the *elephant* feeds, with other animals around him which he defends.

U *before* R.

U-RI'-AS. A principal man among the *jews,* after the babylonifh captivity.

U. *before* T.

U'-TA. One whofe fons were fervants of the temple.

U'-THI. One who returned from the babylonifh captivity.

W.

W.

W *before* A.

WAVE OFFERING. See *Offerings.*

W *before* I.

WITCH. One, who by juggling deludes the fenfes with falfe appearances of things—or one that doth mifchief to man or beaft by evil arts—or a foothfayer. The word in the original is of the feminine gender, becaufe women are fuppofed to be addicted to this crime : but there are men-witches, who are commonly called *wizards.*

WI'Z-ARD. A wizard was one who pretended to confult familiar fpirits, and foretel future events by practifing evil arts.

X.

X.

X *before* A.

XA'N-THI-CUS. A *macedonian* month, anfwering to part of our *February* and part of our *March*.

Z.

Z *before* A.

ZAB-A-DAI'-AS. One who returned fron the babylonifh captivity.

ZA'B-BUD (i. e. *a dowry*; *endowed*) One of the fons of *Bigvai*, who returned from the babylonifh captivity.

ZA'M-BIS. One who returned from the babylonifh captivity.

ZA'-

ZA'-MOTH.   One who returned from the babylonish
captivity.

ZA'-RA (i. e. *rising* ; *clearness*)   One who is mentioned in St. *Matthew's* genealogical lift.

ZA-RAI'-AS (i. e. *the Lord rising*)   An anceftor of
Efdras in the *Apocrypha*.

ZA'-THO-E.   Set *Zatthu*.

ZA'-THU-I.   See *Zatthu*.

Z before E.

ZE'-RAH. (i e. *rising* ; *clearness*)   A fon of *Reuel* a
grandfon to the patriarch *Efau*.

ZE'-RAN.   The father of *Achan*.

Z before I.

ZIB-E-ON.   A wife of the patriarch *Efau*.   See
Zibion.

ZI'CH-RI.   One who defcended from the patriarch
Levi.   See *Zichri* in the Lexicon.

ZI'TH-RI (i. e. *my fecret* ; *my refuge* ; *hid* ; *tumbling
wide*)   One who defcended from the patriarch
Levi.

F I N I S.

ADDITIONS

TO BE MADE TO THE

LEXICON,

IN THE

INTERPRETATION OF NAMES.

AKRABBIM (i. e. *scorpions*)
   Azaliah   (i. e. *near the Lord*)
Asriel   (i. e. *the help of God*)
Baalith   (i. e. *a rejoicing; or proud Lord*)
Bagoas   (i. e. *the inward; most secret; advanced;*
              lifted up)
Bartimeus (i. e. *blind son; or son of blindness*)
Bebai   (i. e. *void, or empty*)
Berith   (i. e. *a covenant*)
Beth Haran (i. e. *the house of an hill*)
Beth Oron (i. e. *the house of anger or of liberty*)
Beth Shure (i. e. *the house of the mouth of the valleys*)
Bileam   (i. e. *the antient of the people; the devourer*)
Boslen   (i. e. *fig barn*)
Cedar   (i. e. *a cart o cross*)
Chirea   (i. e. *build or cold*)
Chloe   (i. e. *green herb*)
Elisabeth ? nn (i. e. *the house of grace or mercy*)
Gazzim   (i. e. *the fleece of them*)
Gitteus   (i. e. *winepresses*)
Hadrach   (i. e. *joy of tenderness*)
Haggith   (i. e. *rejoicing*)
Haradah   (i. e. *the evil of great fear*)
Harhaia   (i. e. *heat or anger of the Lord*)
Hatuch   (i. e. *smiting*)
Hathath   (i. e. *fear*)
Heli   (i. e. *ascending*)

Hit-

Hittites   (i. e. *broken afunder; aftonifhing*)

Jarefiah   (i. e. *the bed of the Lord; the Lord hath taken away; poverty*)

Jehofheba (i. e. *the fulnefs or oath of the Lord; the Lord returning the hour*)

Jethlah   (i. e. *hanging up; heaping up*)

Jorai   (i. e. *declaring; throwing forth; a cauldron*)

Ithrites   (i. e. *excelling; a remaining*)

Izrites   (i. e. *a fafting; tribulation; forrowfull*)

Izharites (i. e. *the fame as Izhar*)

Lemuel   (i. e. *God to them; God with them*)

Lyfia   (i. e. *a wolf*)

Manahethites (i. e. *my lady; my prince of reft*)

Melea   (i. e. *fupplying, or fupplied*)

Menan   (i. e. *numbered; rewarded; prepared*)

Nebuchadnezzar (i. e. *the mourning of the generation; wailing of judgment; forrowing of poverty*)

Nimfhi   (i. e. *refcued from danger; that touches*)

Pharezites (i. e. *divided*)

Samaritans (i. e. *keepers; thorny places; dregs; marvellous herd*)

Shamhuth (i. e. *defolation; perdition; deftroying iniquity*)

Sheminith (i. e. *the eighth*)

Shitrai   (i. e. *a gatherer of mony; a binding; drawn together*)

Silvanus (i. e. *of the wood*)

Simri   (i. e. *a keeping; an adamant ftone; a thorn*)

Spain   (i. e. *rare; precious*)

Suah   (i. e. *rooting up; treading under feet*)

Sufanchites (i. e. *lillies; rofes; the joy of the lame*)

Tigris   (i. e. *the fharpnefs of fwiftnefs; a fharp found; a voice; one only fwiftnefs*)

Ucal   (i. e. *power; prevalence*)

Uzziah   (i. e. *the ftrength of the Lord; the buck-goat of the Lord*)

Zelotes   (i. e. *jealous; full of zeal*)

Zophim   (i. e. *a field where men may fee far off*)

AL.

ALTERATIONS AND ADDITIONS

FOR THE

LEXICON.

UNDER THE NAMES,

BELA. - A king of *Edom*.
Dibri - read *Dan* inftead of *Gad*.
Dorcas - - — *a female roe*.
Elah - - add, *alfo an officer of king Solomon—alfo a fon of Caleb—alfo a duke of Edom*.
Engannim - read, *Judah* inftead of *Iffachar*.
Gathrimmon - — *Dan* inftead of *Ephraim*.
Heth - - - — *fecond fon*.
Jambri. - - A *place* - See *Appendix*.
Jarha - - for *Shefhur*, read, *Shefhan*.
Jemuel - - — *fon of God*, — *fea of God*)
Jephunnah - — *Afher* — *Judah, Caleb's father*
Kohath - read, the *fecond* fon.
Maacah - — *alfo the mother of Abfalom ; one of king David's Concubines*.
Manoah - for *Gad*, read, *Dan*.
Mattan - read, *alfo a prieft of Baal*.
Milcah - for *Aram*, read, *Haran*.
Moza - read, *alfo a fon of Caleb*.
Nicanor - — *alfo a chriftian dæcon*.
Peres - - — *alfo one of king Solomon's captains*.
Rabbah - for *Gad*, read, *Judah*.

Ragau

Ragau - - *A place, suppofed to be in Media, Judith*
chap. i. ver. 5.

Rimmon - read, *a village in the tribe of Simeon*---alfo
the father of Baana and Rechab, two of Saul's
captains.

Thermeleth inftead of a *perfon*, read, a *place.* See
Appendix.

Zatthu - read, *or Zathui.*

Zebaim - — *a place*, inftead of *a perfon.*

Zelah - - for *Ephraim*, read, *Benjamin, where*
king Saul was buried.

Zibion - read, *alfo Efau's wife.*

Zur - - read, *a fo a king of Midian.*

www.ingramcontent.com/pod-product-compliance
Lightning Source LLC
Chambersburg PA
CBHW021522090426
42739CB00007B/731